AGILE SOURCING

YASSER ISMAIL, MCIPS, PMP, PMI-ACP

PASSIONPRENEUR®
P U B L I S H I N G

AGILE SOURCING

The Insider Secrets of Innovative Sourcing

YASSER ISMAIL, MCIPS, PMP, PMI-ACP

PASSIONPRENEUR® PUBLISHING

Publishing information
Publishing and design facilitated by Passionpreneur Publishing
A division of Passionpreneur Organization Pty Ltd
ABN: 48640637529

Melbourne, VIC | Australia
www.PassionpreneurPublishing.com

The book is dedicated to my parents, my family.

TABLE OF CONTENTS

ACKNOWLEDGMENT

I have been fortunate to collaborate with the best teams and leaders around the world throughout the years.

I want to thank all those who assisted me throughout my career and shared their knowledge and expertise.

AGILE SOURCING

*"SMART, INNOVATIVE, AND CREATIVE WAYS
ARE NEEDED TO ACCOMPLISH OUR
OBJECTIVES MORE EFFICIENTLY."*

— YASSER ISMAIL

INTRODUCTION

In recent years, the COVID-19 pandemic has severely affected global supply chains. Many nations implemented quarantine and lockdown measures that disrupted the production and distribution of goods and led to not only product shortages but significant changes in how businesses operate. In addition, border closure and restrictions on international travel made it difficult for companies to transport goods and people to access the products they need. This ripple effect on the global economy highlighted the need for more resilient and flexible supply chain systems.

Our sourcing activities must change and integrate agile methods to meet the needs of clients and organizations.

Depending on the urgency, complexity, and nature of our projects, we need to focus on ways to deliver projects faster to meet current and future challenges. To meet this challenge, sourcing managers can no longer apply a fixed approach to the project management of sourcing projects—each project is unique. Implementing flexible project management tools and techniques, and agile methodologies, will improve the chances of delivering successful projects and opening new opportunities.

This book highlights agile values and principles and recommends a mix of agile and traditional waterfall methods. It will serve as a guide or reference for sourcing and procurement managers, sourcing specialists, entrepreneurs, and people involved in sourcing tenders, regardless of their commodities or categories.

From initiation through to concluding and handing the contract over to the supplier manager, I outline the best practices for project management. The right method will depend on the situation and its urgency—every project has its unique scope, risks, stakeholders, and environment. I aim to demonstrate how agile methodologies and project management can combine previous experience and knowledge to enhance sourcing and tendering processes.

Our careers unfold in stages of growing confidence and ability. Working in a multinational environment is like playing in an orchestra made up of many instruments, shapes, and notes—it provides an ideal space for learning and collaboration. Through our interactions, we are enriched and influenced by contributions from people from diverse cultures.

I developed this book based on my experience as a sourcing professional, a Project Management Professional (PMP), and a PMI Agile Certified Practitioner (PMI-ACP).

AGILE METHODOLOGIES

This book aims to show how agile approaches can be used to deliver a range of successful projects, including, but not limited to, software development. The most appropriate approach will depend on the nature of the project.

Agile methodologies are useful when working on projects with a rapid turnaround, while the waterfall method is recommended when there is no scope for agile methodologies or if the price and quality are close to matching.[1]

An agile–waterfall hybrid approach is beneficial for projects that will take more than four weeks to complete.

FACT: THE WATERFALL METHOD IS RECOMMENDED WHEN THERE IS NO SCOPE FOR AGILE METHODOLOGIES OR IF THE PRICE AND QUALITY ARE CLOSE TO MATCHING.

WHAT IS AGILE PROJECT MANAGEMENT?

An agile project management approach emphasizes flexibility, collaboration, and continuous improvement. Software development is a key area where agile methodologies can be effectively applied, along with sourcing and procurement.

---

1   Source: https://www.guru99.com/waterfall-vs-agile.html.

Procurement and sourcing organizations can benefit from agile practices by adapting quickly and effectively to changing market conditions and customer needs.

HOW DO THE AGILE AND WATERFALL APPROACHES DIFFER?

Understanding the key elements of the agile and waterfall methodologies will allow you to deliver projects more effectively:

- An agile approach is iterative and incremental, while a waterfall approach is linear and sequential.
- An agile approach divides a project into sprints, while a waterfall approach divides a project into phases.
- An agile approach helps complete small projects, while a waterfall approach helps complete a single project.
- When taking an agile approach, the project scope and requirements can be changed at any time. Scope changes should be avoided in the waterfall approach and a pre-set plan should be followed.
- In agile project management, team members are responsible for developing the project. In contrast, a project manager oversees every project phase in waterfall project management.
- An agile approach aims to deliver products that satisfy customers, while a waterfall approach aims to successfully attain agreed goals.

THE HISTORY OF THE AGILE APPROACH

Agile software development is a set of values and principles for software development that emphasizes collaboration, adaptability, and flexibility. Agile teams aim to deliver high-quality software quickly and efficiently by working collaboratively and iteratively.[2]

> *FACT: AGILE SOFTWARE DEVELOPMENT IS BASED ON A SET OF VALUES AND PRINCIPLES THAT EMPHASIZE COLLABORATION, ADAPTABILITY, AND FLEXIBILITY.*

These values guide agile teams and help them focus on delivering value to their customers. Agile teams aim to deliver working software regularly, welcome and incorporate change, and collaborate with customers and stakeholders.

In the spring of 2001, seventeen software developers met in Oregon in the United States to discuss ways to reduce development times:

Kent Beck	James Grenning	Robert C. Martin
Mike Beedle	Jim Highsmith	Steve Mellor
Arie van Bennekum	Andrew Hunt	Ken Schwaber
Alistair Cockburn	Ron Jeffries	Jeff Sutherland
Ward Cunningham	Jon Kern	Dave Thomas
Martin Fowler	Brian Marick	

---

2   Source: https://www.techtarget.com/searchsoftwarequality/definition/agile-software-development.

They recognized two key opportunities that would result from achieving this goal:

1. shortening the time to provide benefits to users to resolve product–market fit issues and develop graveyards
2. getting user feedback quickly for the continuous improvement of new software.[3]

FACT: RESOLVING PRODUCT–MARKET FIT ISSUES AND DEVELOPING GRAVEYARDS INVOLVES SHORTENING THE TIME TO PROVIDE BENEFITS TO USERS.

This meeting was crucial for today's agile methodology, as speed, rapid feedback, and continual improvement are hallmarks of an agile method.

MANIFESTO FOR AGILE SOFTWARE DEVELOPMENT

We are uncovering better ways of developing software by doing it and helping others do it. Through this work, we have come to value:

- individuals and interactions over processes and tools
- working software over comprehensive documentation

---

3   Source: https://www.planview.com/resources/guide/agile-methodologies-a-beginners-guide/history-of-agile/.

- customer collaboration over contract negotiation
- responding to change over following a plan.

While there is value in all these concepts, we value the agile focus items more highly.

PRINCIPLES BEHIND THE AGILE MANIFESTO

1. Our highest priority is to satisfy the customer through early and continuous delivery of valuable software.
2. Welcome changing requirements, even late in development. Agile processes harness change for the customer's competitive advantage.
3. Deliver working software frequently, from a couple of weeks to a couple of months, with a preference to the shorter timescale.
4. Business people and developers must work together daily throughout the project.
5. Build projects around motivated individuals. Give them the environment and support they need and trust them to get the job done.
6. The most efficient and effective method of conveying information to and within a development team is face-to-face conversation.
7. Working software is the primary measure of progress.
8. Agile processes promote sustainable development. The sponsors, developers, and users should be able to maintain a constant pace indefinitely.

9. Continuous attention to technical excellence and good design enhances agility.
10. Simplicity—the art of maximizing the amount of work not done—is essential.
11. The best architecture, requirements, and designs emerge from self-organizing teams.
12. At regular intervals, the team reflects on how to become more effective, then tunes and adjusts its behavior accordingly.[4]

THE IMPORTANCE OF AGILE SOURCING

During challenging periods, it is crucial to deliver projects faster. An agile method, or a hybrid model of both predictive and agile methods, is suitable for projects that must be delivered within one to four weeks.

Examples of the use of agile principles and practices in procurement and sourcing activities include:

Rapid prototyping: Agile sourcing can help procurement teams prototype and test new products or services before committing to a long-term contract and help teams identify potential issues early and make necessary adjustments.

Continuous improvement: Agile sourcing can support continuous improvement by allowing teams to regularly review their performance and identify opportunities for improvement.

---

4   Source: http://agilemanifesto.org/iso/en/principles.html.

Flexibility: Agile sourcing can help procurement teams be more flexible in their sourcing approach, allowing them to adapt quickly to changing market conditions and customer needs.

Collaboration: Agile sourcing can support collaboration between procurement and other teams within an organization, allowing teams to work together to identify and address issues on time.

Time-to-market: Agile sourcing can help organizations reduce the time taken to bring new products or services to market by streamlining the procurement process and enabling teams to make decisions quickly.

HOW AGILE METHODOLOGIES WORK FOR PROCUREMENT AND SOURCING

An agile approach can help procurement and sourcing teams to work more closely with other departments and stakeholders.

By involving all relevant parties in the decision-making process, agile approaches can ensure that procurement and sourcing strategies align with the overall goals and priorities of the organization.

An agile project management approach emphasizes flexibility, collaboration, and continuous improvement.

In the context of procurement and sourcing, agile approaches can help organizations adapt promptly and effectively to changing market conditions and customer needs.

In traditional procurement and sourcing processes, teams often operate in silos, with little coordination or cooperation with other parts of the organization. An agile approach can help procurement and sourcing teams to collaborate closely with other departments and stakeholders by involving all relevant parties in the decision-making process. For example, a procurement and sourcing team might use agile methods such as daily stand-up meetings and retrospectives to regularly review their performance and identify areas for improvement.

An example of a project calling for agile methodologies is when a company is looking to source a new component for its manufacturing process. The procurement team might identify a potential supplier and negotiate a contract without consulting other departments in a traditional procurement and sourcing process. However, using agile methods, the procurement and sourcing team would involve the engineering department in decision-making. The engineering team could then provide input on the technical requirements of the component, and the procurement and sourcing team could use this information to identify the most suitable supplier and negotiate a contract that aligns with the organization's overall goals.

Agile methodologies can be incorporated into procurement and sourcing, aligning procurement tactics with organizational objectives and involving all relevant stakeholders. By adopting agile principles and practices, organizations can improve their performance and better support the needs of their customers and stakeholders, focusing on collaboration, flexibility, and continuous improvement.

CHAPTER 1

SOURCING OVERVIEW

PROCUREMENT
*IS THE PROCESS OF GETTING
THE MATERIALS NEEDED.*
SOURCING
*IS FINDING AND VETTING THE SUPPLIERS
OF THOSE MATERIALS.*

HOW DO PROCUREMENT AND SOURCING DIFFER?

Procurement and sourcing are distinct processes that are often confused. Although they are related, they are not the same.

Procurement is the process of obtaining goods and services from outside sources. It involves identifying the need for a product or service, researching potential suppliers, negotiating contracts, and managing the purchase process. Procurement also includes managing the delivery of the goods or services, ensuring quality, and managing the payment process.

On the other hand, sourcing involves finding and evaluating potential suppliers. It involves researching potential suppliers, evaluating their capabilities, and selecting the best supplier for the job. Sourcing also involves negotiating contracts, managing the supplier relationship, and ensuring that the supplier meets the organization's needs.

The main difference between procurement and sourcing is that procurement is focused on the purchase process, while sourcing is focused on potential suppliers. Procurement is more focused on the transaction, while sourcing is more focused on relationships.

Procurement and sourcing are important processes for any organization. They help ensure that the organization gets the best value for money and that the goods and services it purchases are of the highest quality. By understanding the differences between procurement and sourcing, organizations can ensure they make the best decisions for their business.

In summary, procurement and sourcing have the following differences:

Purpose: In procurement, goods and services are acquired, whereas in sourcing, vendors or suppliers are identified and selected to provide those goods and services.

Scope: In general, procurement involves the complete process of acquiring goods and services, from identifying the need to completing the contract and making the payment. Alternatively, sourcing is concerned with identifying and selecting vendors and suppliers.

Focus: In procurement, contracting and negotiations are concentrated on acquiring goods and services. Sourcing primarily focuses on identifying the best sources of supply and developing long-term relationships with suppliers and vendors.

Increasing profits involves reducing material expenses while maintaining quality standards, as customer satisfaction is paramount. Cutting costs by using defective materials can lead to inferior products, which ultimately contradicts the objective of meeting customer expectations. Before sourcing begins, assess your purchasing needs, conduct marketing research, and identify potential suppliers. Once completed, evaluate the suppliers to choose the most suitable match for your requirement. Then, repeat this method for all purchasing needs.

PROJECT MANAGEMENT

Managing a project involves applying knowledge, skills, tools, and techniques to achieve specific targets within specified budgets and time constraints.

Scope: What work is and is not included in the project.

Time: The amount of time needed to complete the project.

Cost: Based on the time to complete the project multiplied by the cost of human resources necessary to complete the project.

Quality: Indicates how successful the results of a project are—satisfies the objective specified by management.

SOURCING PROJECT DEFINITION

A project is an initiative to produce a unique result, product, or service.

Sourcing projects are well-defined. They have a start and end date and are launched to source products or services from qualified or approved suppliers or service providers. The project ends as soon as the contract is awarded and handed over to the supplier manager or project requester.

A successful sourcing project will satisfy stakeholder needs and increase the probability of the final delivery of products or services to clients by meeting deadlines at the correct cost and quality, achieving the organization's goals, and enabling the creation of business value.

WHO REQUESTS THE PROJECT?

A project may be started by a request from within or outside the organization.

Sourcing projects start with a request from any team member of a department within the organization, or they can be initiated directly by a sourcing department after performing a spend analysis of various categories and targeting high-spend commodities. The requester must have the power to order the products or services or obtain approval from a person authorized to approve the request.

The aims of the project must be clear—it could be for internal use by the organization, such as for the improvement of products or innovative technology, for external clients' products or services, or to meet legal or environmental needs.

BUSINESS VALUE

Business value is not necessarily related to money—it could address one of the following values:

- meet customer requirements and satisfaction
- improve processes, products, or services
- social and community
- increase revenue
- innovations and digital transformation.

PROJECT SPONSOR

Project sponsors are people or organizations who provide resources and support for the project, program, or portfolio to succeed.

As necessary, the project sponsor evaluates progress against project plans and provides feedback to the project manager.

Additionally, sponsors support the project manager and their team to work autonomously while ensuring processes are followed.

PROJECT STAKEHOLDERS

Stakeholders may be internal or external. Failure to identify all the project stakeholders may lead to project cancellation, delayed approvals during the project life cycle, or project rejections at closure.

Internal stakeholders include top management, team members, managers, supervisors, senior executives, shareholders, alliance partners, and internal customers.

External stakeholders include clients, subcontractors, manufacturers, government agencies, trade associations, and the public.

Identify project stakeholders with the following questions:

- Who is interested in the project's success?
- Who will you consult before you start implementing your project?
- Who will be affected by the project?
- What external groups or organizations are affected by the project?
- Who can influence the project but is not directly involved?
- Who will support change?
- Are there specific people you need to contact?
- Who might be opposed to change?
- Does making the change have any political, environmental, or social consequences? Who will be affected?

PROJECT MANAGER

The project manager is responsible for ensuring a project is delivered to specification, on time, and within budget. Project managers must coordinate the activities of specialists.

THE ROLE OF THE SOURCING MANAGER

The sourcing manager plays a vital role in supporting other project managers by sourcing the materials and supplies or services required to meet deadlines for deliverables.

The sourcing manager is considered the project manager who manages the company's end-to-end sourcing operations.

WATERFALL SOURCING PROJECT LIFE CYCLE

According to the project complexity, there are five stages in the project life cycle; this could take from one month to six months or more.

1. **Initiation:** Understand the goals; create a business case; complete the project charter, priorities, deadlines, and risks of the project; define stakeholders.
2. **Planning:** Define the scope and outline the tasks and timeline required to execute the project.
3. **Execution:** Implement your plan and monitor your project's progress.
4. **Monitoring and controlling:** Track project progress, ensure adherence to the plan, and prevent disruptions.
5. **Closure:** Analyze results, summarize critical learnings, plan next steps, and hand over the contract to the supplier manager.

THE AGILE DEVELOPMENT CYCLE

Here are the phases in the agile development cycle. It is important to note that these phases should not occur in succession; they are flexible and constantly evolving—they occur in parallel.

1. **Planning:** Once an idea is deemed viable and feasible, the project team comes together and works to identify features. This phase aims to break down the concept into smaller pieces of work (the features), then prioritize each feature and assign it to an iteration.
2. **Requirement analysis:** This phase involves meetings with managers, stakeholders, and users to identify business requirements. The team needs to gather information like who will use the product and how they will use it. These requirements must be quantifiable, relevant, and detailed.
3. **Design:** The system and software design are prepared from the requirements identified in the previous phase. The team needs to think about what the product or solution will look like. The test team also produces a test strategy or plan to proceed.
4. **Implementation:** This phase is about creating and testing features and scheduling iterations for deployment (following the iterative and incremental development approach [IID]). The development phase starts with iteration zero because their features are being viewed. This iteration lays down the foundation for development, with

tasks like finalizing contracts, preparing the environments, and funding.

5. **Testing:** Once the code has been developed, it is evaluated against the requirements to ensure the product addresses customer needs and matches user stories. Unit testing, integration testing, system testing, and acceptance testing are undertaken during this deployment phase. After testing, the product is delivered to customers for use. However, this is not the end of the project. Once customers start using the product, they may encounter problems that the project team will need to address.

METHODOLOGIES USED TO IMPLEMENT AGILE FRAMEWORK

Specific methods exist within the agile movement. These can be thought of as different flavors. Only two of these will be presented here:

Kanban: Kanban, meaning "visual sign" or "card" in Japanese, is a framework for implementing an agile approach. It promotes small, continuous changes to your current system. Its principles include visualizing the workflow, limiting work in progress, managing and enhancing the flow, making policies explicit, and continuously improving.

Scrum: Scrum is one of the most popular ways to implement an agile approach. It is an iterative software model that follows a set of roles, responsibilities, and meetings that never change. Sprints, usually lasting one to two weeks, allow the team to deliver software regularly.

When it comes to sourcing and procurement projects, Scrum and Kanban can be used to help teams stay organized and on track.

With Scrum, teams can break down complex tasks into smaller, more manageable chunks to allow teams to focus on each task separately and ensure that each task is completed before moving on to the next one. Scrum also encourages collaboration and communication between team members, which can help ensure everyone works toward the same goal.

Kanban can also be used to help teams manage their workflow.

By visualizing tasks and workflows, teams can easily prioritize and ensure they are working on the most important tasks, helping them stay organized and on track and ensuring that procurement and sourcing tasks are completed on time.

CHAPTER 2

PROJECT INITIATION

A PROJECT'S INITIATION IS IMPERATIVE SINCE IT MUST JUSTIFY ITS OUTCOME. CHOOSING THE RIGHT PROJECT OR STARTING IT PROPERLY CAN SAVE TIME AND COMPROMISE.

INTRODUCTION

Project initiation involves defining and documenting a project's scope, objectives, and stakeholders in the first phase of its lifecycle.

This phase establishes the foundation for the rest of the project and ensures it remains on track.

The project team will develop a project charter during the project initiation phase. Goals, objectives, stakeholders, and a high-level plan for executing the project are described in this document.

Following the initiation phase, the planning phase will result in the development of a more detailed plan, and the project manager will form the project team.

During this phase, the project team will typically perform the following activities:

Identify the project's goals and objectives: Project initiation begins with defining the project's goals and objectives and ensuring everyone understands them. This will typically involve conducting stakeholder interviews and workshops to gather input and feedback on the project's goals and objectives.

Prepare a project charter: This document outlines the project's goals, objectives, and stakeholders, and describes how it will be executed on a high level. The project charter should be developed with all relevant stakeholders, and it should be reviewed and approved by the project sponsor before moving forward.

Identify project constraints and assumptions: To develop a realistic plan for the project, it is essential to identify any constraints or assumptions that may impact the project. This could include factors such as budget, timeline, and available resources, as well as any assumptions that have been made about the project's scope or requirements.

Develop a high-level project plan: Based on the project charter and any identified constraints or assumptions, the project team will develop a high-level plan for the project. This plan should include a broad overview of the project's scope and objectives and a timeline for key milestones and deliverables.

Assemble the project team: In the project initiation phase, the team will typically be assembled and provide an overview of the project's goals and objectives. This is an opportunity for the team to become familiar with the project and to begin planning how they will contribute to its success.

Overall, the project initiation phase is crucial in the project lifecycle. It helps define the project's scope, objectives, and stakeholders, and it sets the foundations for the rest of the project. By ensuring that the project is initiated correctly, the project team can increase the likelihood of success and reduce the risk of issues or delays later in the project.

BUSINESS DOCUMENTS

During the project phases, various documents are used. The business documents created before the project are reviewed periodically.

Business case: A business case is presented to show whether the expected outcome of a project justifies the required investment; it is created in response to an organizational need or a customer request.

The project sponsor usually creates it or delegates it to the project manager; it is considered the primary document from which the project charter is developed.

The project manager needs to update or change these documents because they are projected; however, they can make recommendations.

Project charter: A project charter is the birth certificate of a project; it includes the necessary information from the business documents.

Agreements: Agreements are used to trigger the purpose for the initiation of the project.

Agreements have different forms of contracts, memorandums of understanding (MOUs), service level agreements (SLA), verbal agreements, letters of intent, letters of agreement, e-mails, and any other written agreements with an external customer.

ENTERPRISE ENVIRONMENTAL FACTORS (EEF)

EEF can significantly impact the development of project charters, which is the first phase of project management. The project charter defines the objectives, scope, stakeholders, risks, and other important aspects of a project, and it serves as a basis for project planning and execution. It includes, but is not limited to:

- government or industry standards (e.g., product standards, quality standards, safety standards, and quality standards)
- legal and regulatory requirements and or constraints
- marketplace conditions
- organizational culture and political climate
- organizational governance framework (a structured way to provide control, direction, and coordination through people, policies, and processes to meet organizational strategic and operational goals)
- stakeholders' expectations and risk thresholds.

ORGANIZATIONAL PROCESS ASSETS

A project charter can be developed on the strengths of the organization's process, including the following:

- organizational standard policies, processes, and procedures
- portfolio, program, and project governance framework (governance functions and processes to provide guidance and decision-making)

- monitoring and reporting methods
- templates (e.g., project charter template)
- historical information and lessons learned repository (e.g., project records and documents, information about the results of previous project selection decisions, and information about last project performance).

DATA GATHERING

The sourcing manager utilizes the following tools to gather all the information related to the project:

Expert judgement: As part of the project planning process, judgments are made based on skill, expertise, or specialized knowledge in each area. Training, education, experiences, and product/market understanding contribute to their expertise.

Interpersonal and team skills: Interpersonal and team skills describe an individual's behaviors and tactics for successfully interacting with stakeholders. Developing and maintaining relationships with others is crucial to the project's success.

Meetings: Meetings with project participants and stakeholders are about communicating, discussing issues, presenting proposals, and approving or rejecting them.

Group decisions accelerate project delivery by providing planned goals and expected outcomes.

Stakeholders: Business stakeholders can either affect the business or be affected by it; they are allies of the business.

Investors, employees, customers, and suppliers are the primary stakeholders in a typical corporation.

STAKEHOLDER MANAGEMENT

Identifying all stakeholders is critical to the success of any project. During the project, the stakeholder register must be kept up to date; missing crucial stakeholders could result in the failure or cancellation of the project. After the stakeholders have been identified, they should be classified based on their interests and influence.

Project management means ensuring that all stakeholders are involved and providing support and collaboration during the project. If a stakeholder loses interest, they should be reminded of the importance of the project. Influential stakeholders should be kept informed through periodical updates and continued engagement.

IMPLEMENTING AGILE PRINCIPLES DURING INITIATION

It is recommended that the following principles be upheld during the initiation phase:

Individuals and interactions over processes and tools: It is essential to build trust and collaboration channels with key individuals and project stakeholders to ensure that they will be willing to commit to each stage until the end of the project, as they are essential to collecting all the necessary information and completing the scope of work.

Respond to change by following a plan: It is critical to welcome changes in requirements, even late in the development process, from the initiation phase to the closing phase.

An agile methodology harnesses change for the customer's competitive advantage.

Maintain continuity of delivery and provide customer satisfaction as early as possible: Starting with the initiation phase, you should turn over the project as soon as possible by completing every phase as quickly as possible.

Work together: The project team and stakeholders must work together. The project team must stay on top of the project and regularly communicate progress to the stakeholders.

Motivate individuals: Motivated individuals should be at the center of your projects. It is essential that these individuals are equipped with the right tools and support, and they should be trusted to do the job. In this way, team members will realize their contribution is valued and appreciated, and this will motivate them significantly.

Motivating individuals on a development team as part of an agile philosophy is imperative. By allowing the team to self-organize and self-control, you can maximize this motivation.

Members of a self-organizing development team choose the specific tasks they would like to work on instead of being dictated to (micro-managed).

Face-to-face conversation: The most efficient and effective method of conveying information to and within a project team is face-to-face conversation. Face-to-face communication lets the other person see how your actions align with your words, and this enhances your credibility.

STARTING A PROJECT

The sourcing lead or manager will collect all the following documents and prepare a summary document called the "minimum facts," which summarizes the documents required to start a sourcing project. This will vary depending on the project's particular nature and the organization's needs. However, standard documents that may be required for an agile procurement and sourcing project include the following:

A project charter: This provides a high-level overview of the project's scope, objectives, and key stakeholders and provides a high-level overview of the project's plan and timeline.

A project plan: This document provides a detailed roadmap, including the specific tasks, milestones, and deliverables that will be completed.

A requirements document: This document outlines the specific requirements and constraints for the project, including the goods or services that will be procured, the budget, and any other constraints or considerations.

A sourcing or procurement plan: This document outlines the specific sourcing processes and procedures used, including the methods for identifying and evaluating potential vendors or suppliers and the criteria used to select the best option.

A contract: Once a supplier has been selected, a contract will be required to outline the terms and conditions of the agreement, including the scope of work, the price, and any other relevant details.

Overall, the documents required for an agile procurement and sourcing project will vary depending on the organization's needs and the project's scope. However, standard documents include a project charter, a project plan, a requirements document, a procurement plan, and a contract. These documents help to provide structure and guidance for the project and ensure that it is conducted effectively and efficiently.

CHAPTER 3

PROJECT PLANNING

"ESSENTIALLY ALL MODELS ARE WRONG,
BUT SOME ARE USEFUL."

— GEORGE E. P. BOX (1976)

EVERY PROJECT IS UNIQUE

You cannot apply a one-size-fits-all approach to sourcing. A team may tailor the process according to its needs and the unique circumstances in which it operates.

The procurement and sourcing process involves acquiring goods and services for a company. An agile approach to project planning emphasizes flexibility, collaboration, and the ability to adapt quickly to changing conditions or requirements.

When using agile practices for procurement and sourcing, the project team will begin by identifying the needed goods and services and then collaborating with stakeholders to establish priorities and define the project's scope. The team will then create a high-level plan for acquiring the goods and services and break the plan down into smaller, manageable chunks called "iterations" or "sprints."

During each iteration or sprint, the team will identify and evaluate potential suppliers, solicit bids or proposals, and decide which suppliers to engage. The project's goals will be achieved by tracking progress and adjusting plans as necessary.

By using agile methods, procurement and sourcing teams can be more responsive to changing requirements or priorities. They can better manage the risks and complexities often associated with acquiring goods and services.

Establish priorities and define the project's scope: Once the needed goods and services have been identified, the team will collaborate with stakeholders to establish priorities and define the project's boundaries. This involves determining which goods and services are essential and defining the constraints and limitations that will shape the project's approach and direction.

Create a high-level plan: Based on the priorities and scope, the team will create a high-level plan for acquiring the goods and services that are needed. This plan provides a broad overview of the steps that will be taken to acquire the goods and services and serves as a roadmap for the project.

Break the plan down into iterations or sprints: The high-level plan is then broken down into smaller, manageable chunks (iterations or sprints). Each iteration or sprint involves specific tasks and activities focused on acquiring a particular group of goods and services.

Identify and evaluate potential suppliers: During each iteration or sprint, the team will work together to identify potential suppliers for the needed goods and services. This might involve researching, reaching out to industry contacts, or using other methods to identify potential suppliers.

Once potential suppliers have been identified, the team can evaluate them to determine the most qualified and capable of meeting the organization's needs.

Solicit bids or proposals: Once potential suppliers have been identified and evaluated, the team solicits bids or proposals from the most qualified suppliers. This involves providing the suppliers with detailed information about the needed goods and services and asking them to submit a proposal outlining how they would fulfill the organization's needs.

Decide which suppliers to engage: After bids or proposals have been received, the team will review and evaluate them to determine which suppliers are most qualified and capable of fulfilling the organization's needs. The team will then decide which suppliers to engage and begin negotiating contracts and finalizing the arrangements for the acquisition of the goods and services.

Track progress and adjust the plan as needed: Throughout the project, the team will track progress and monitor key performance indicators to ensure that the project stays on track and meets its objectives. If necessary, the team will adjust the plan and amend the project's approach to keep it on track and ensure it is successful.

SCOPE MANAGEMENT PLAN

As stated earlier, when using agile methods for procurement and sourcing, the project team will begin by defining the project's scope. This involves collaborating with stakeholders to understand the organization's needs and requirements and determining which goods and services are necessary to meet those needs.

Once the needed goods and services have been identified, the team establishes priorities and defines the project's boundaries. This involves deciding which goods and services are essential and defining the constraints and limitations that will shape the project's approach and direction.

The team will then create a high-level plan for acquiring the needed goods and services and break the plan down into iterations or sprints. Each iteration or sprint involves specific tasks and activities focused on acquiring a particular group of goods and services.

In this way, the team can ensure that the project stays focused and that they can deliver the goods and services that are needed in a timely and effective manner. This approach also allows the team to be more responsive to changing requirements or priorities and adjust the project's scope (as needed) to ensure success.

The project scope describes what goods and services will be acquired and how. Defining the project's scope is a crucial step in the planning process because it helps the project team understand the organization's needs and requirements. The scope of a procurement and sourcing project might include the following:

- the types of needed goods and services, such as raw materials, finished goods, or services (e.g., consulting or support)
- the number of needed goods and services, such as the units or services that will be required

- the timeframe for acquiring the goods and services, such as the deadlines for completing each iteration or sprint or the overall project deadline
- the budget for acquiring the goods and services, such as the total amount of money available for the project or the maximum amount that can be spent on each iteration or sprint
- the criteria for selecting suppliers, such as the qualifications or experience, or the standards suppliers must meet in order to be chosen.

By defining the project's scope, the project team can ensure that it is clear about what needs to be done and can focus its efforts on acquiring the goods and services necessary to meet the organization's needs. This can increase the project's success and efficiency and reduce the risk of delays or problems.

EXAMPLE OF THE SCOPE OF WORK FOR "DOMESTIC TRUCKS"

The scope of work for a tender of domestic trucks should outline the requirements and specifications for the trucks being purchased, as well as the terms and conditions of the tender process. Here are the key elements that could be included in a scope of work for a tender of domestic trucks:

Description of the trucks: This should include information on the make, model, and size of the trucks being purchased, as well as any specific features or requirements (e.g., refrigeration, lift gates).

Delivery and installation: The scope of work should specify where the trucks will be delivered and whether installation or other additional services are required.

Pricing and payment terms: This should include details on how the trucks will be priced (e.g., per unit, as a package), as well as information on any discounts or incentives that may be offered. The scope of work should also outline the truck payment terms, including any deposit or down-payment requirements.

Warranty and maintenance: The scope of work should specify the terms of any warranties or maintenance agreements included with the trucks, including the duration of the warranties and any exclusions or limitations.

Evaluation criteria: A scope of work should stipulate what factors will be considered when evaluating the bids submitted in a tender process. Examples include price, delivery time, and overall truck quality.

Service and support: The scope of work may include information on the level of service and support—including details on spare parts availability, technical assistance, and any other relevant services—that the supplier will provide.

Training: If training is required for the trucks being purchased, the scope of work should outline the type and duration of training that will be provided and any costs associated with the training.

Environmental considerations: Businesses may have specific environmental or sustainability goals they want to achieve through their truck purchases. The scope of work could include information on any environmental standards or requirements the trucks must meet.

Customization: If the purchased trucks need to be customized to meet specific business needs, the scope of work should outline the customization requirements and associated costs.

Compliance: The scope of work should specify any regulatory or compliance requirements that the trucks must meet (e.g., safety standards, emission regulations).

By including these additional elements in the scope of work, businesses can ensure that they receive detailed and comprehensive information from potential suppliers and can make informed decisions when selecting a supplier for their domestic truck needs.

COLLECT REQUIREMENTS

Collecting requirements involves gathering information about the organization's needs and requirements and using that information to plan and execute the project.

There are key steps involved in collecting requirements for a procurement and sourcing project:

Identify stakeholders: The first step in collecting requirements is to identify the stakeholders who will be affected by the project or have a personal stake in its success. This might include department managers, users of the goods and services, or other parties who will be involved in the project.

Engage with stakeholders: Once stakeholders have been identified, the project team should engage with them to gather information about their needs and requirements. This might involve conducting interviews, surveys, or workshops to gather input and feedback from stakeholders.

Document requirements: As information is gathered from stakeholders, it should be carefully documented and organized. This might involve creating a requirements document or database that lists each stakeholder's specific needs and requirements, along with any constraints or limitations that need to be considered.

Validate requirements: Once the requirements have been documented, the project team should validate them to ensure that they are accurate and complete. This might involve conducting additional research or seeking other input or feedback from stakeholders.

By collecting requirements and engaging with stakeholders, the project team can ensure that it has a clear understanding of the organization's needs and requirements and can plan and execute the project accordingly.

SCHEDULE MANAGEMENT PLAN

By breaking the project down into smaller, manageable chunks, the project team is able to create a schedule. Each iteration or sprint involves specific tasks and activities focused on acquiring a particular group of goods and services.

The team will then plan the schedule for each iteration or sprint, considering factors such as the availability of resources, the time needed to complete each task, and any dependencies or constraints that must be considered. The team will also establish deadlines for each iteration or sprint and track progress to ensure the project is on track.

When a project is broken down into smaller chunks, the project team is more flexible and responsive to changing requirements and priorities. Additionally, the team can adjust the schedule to ensure the project stays on track and amend the project's approach if necessary. Project success and efficiency can be improved, and delays and problems can be reduced.

The project team will create a schedule by defining the activities that need to be completed and then sequencing those activities in the most effective order. To define the activities for a procurement and sourcing project, the team will first identify the needed goods and services, then determine the necessary steps to acquire those goods and services. This might involve researching, evaluating potential suppliers, soliciting bids or proposals, or negotiating contracts.

Once the activities have been defined, the team will sequence them in the most effective order. This might involve organizing the activities into a logical sequence or grouping them into iterations or sprints. The team will also consider factors such as the availability of resources, the time needed to complete each activity, and any dependencies or constraints that must be considered.

After the activities have been defined and sequenced, the team will estimate the duration of each activity, considering factors such as the complexity of the task, the availability of resources, and any uncertainties or risks that might affect the project.

Based on the estimated duration of the activities, the team will then develop a schedule for the project, specifying the start and end dates for each iteration or sprint and outlining the activities that will be completed during each one. Schedule adjustment, where necessary, will ensure that the project stays on track and meets its goals.

COST MANAGEMENT PLAN

The project team will create a cost plan by estimating the needed goods and services, then developing a budget for the project.

To estimate the costs of the needed goods and services, the team will first identify the required goods and services and then determine the quantity of each needed. The team will then research the market to determine the typical prices for the goods and services and use that information to determine the total cost of acquiring the goods and services.

Based on the estimated costs of the goods and services, the team will develop a budget for the project, considering factors such as the availability of funds, the priorities and goals of the organization, and any constraints or limitations that must be considered. The team will also establish guidelines and controls for managing the project's budget and track and monitor its costs to ensure they remain within the budget.

For example, suppose the project requires a certain quantity of raw materials. In that case, the team might research the prices of those materials from different suppliers and use that information to estimate the total cost of acquiring the materials. The team might also consider other factors that could affect the cost, such as transportation costs, taxes, or additional fees.

The team will then develop a project budget based on the estimated costs of the goods and services. The budget specifies the amount of money available for the project and outlines how that money will be allocated to different activities or iterations. The team will establish guidelines and controls for managing the project's budget and track and monitor any spending.

By creating a cost plan and a budget for the project, the project team can ensure that it is financially feasible and has the resources it needs to succeed. This can help the project be more efficient and effective and reduce the risk of delays or problems.

QUALITY MANAGEMENT PLAN

The project team will create a quality plan by defining the standards and criteria that will be used to ensure that the goods and services that are acquired are of a high quality.

To create a quality plan, the team will first identify the needed goods and services and establish the standards and evaluation criteria for the quality of these goods and services. This might involve defining specific performance or reliability standards or establishing requirements for the suppliers providing the goods and services.

The team will then develop a plan to ensure that the acquired goods and services meet the established quality standards. This might involve conducting inspections or tests or implementing other quality control measures. The team will also establish processes for tracking and monitoring the quality of the goods and services and adjust the project's approach, if necessary, to ensure that the quality objectives are met.

By creating a quality plan, the project team can ensure that the goods and services acquired are of a high quality and will meet the organization's needs and requirements. This can help the project be more successful and efficient and reduce the risk of delays or problems.

When using agile methods for procurement and sourcing, the project team will set up quality metrics as part of the quality plan. Quality metrics are measures or indicators used to evaluate the quality of goods and services. These metrics might include measures such as:

- the percentage of goods and services that meet or exceed the established quality standards
- the number of defects or deficiencies in the goods and services acquired
- the number of complaints, issues, or customers of the goods and services
- the level of satisfaction or acceptance of the goods and services by users or customers.

Fixing or addressing issues with the quality of goods and services may take considerable time or resources.

RESOURCE MANAGEMENT PLAN

The project team will create a resource plan by identifying the people, equipment, and other resources needed to complete the project, then determining how those resources will be obtained and managed.

The team will first identify the required activities and tasks to create a resource plan to acquire the goods and services. It will then determine the people, equipment, and other resources required to complete those activities and tasks. This might involve collaborating with stakeholders to understand their needs and requirements or researching the best approach for acquiring the resources.

Once the needed resources have been identified, the team will develop a plan for obtaining and managing those resources. This might involve securing funding or other support from the organization or negotiating contracts or agreements with suppliers or vendors. The team will also establish processes for tracking and managing the project's resources.

By creating a resource plan, the project team can ensure that the project has the people, equipment, and other resources needed to succeed. This can help the project to be more efficient and effective and prevent delays or problems.

The project team will estimate the resources needed for each activity by considering the activity's scope, complexity, and duration. First, they will identify the people, equipment, and other resources required to complete the activity. This might involve conducting research on the most effective approach for acquiring the resources or consulting with stakeholders to understand their needs and requirements.

The team will then estimate the quantity of each needed resource based on factors such as the activity's scope, the task's complexity, and the amount of time available to complete the activity. The team might also consider factors such as the availability of resources, the cost of acquiring the resources, and any constraints or limitations that must be considered.

Based on the estimated quantities of the needed resources, the team will develop a plan for obtaining and managing those resources. This might involve securing funding or other support from the organization or negotiating contracts or agreements with suppliers or vendors. The team will also establish processes for tracking and managing the project's resources and adjust the project's approach, if necessary, to ensure that the project's resource objectives are met.

COMMUNICATIONS MANAGEMENT PLAN

The project team will create a communications plan by identifying the stakeholders who need to be involved in the project, then developing a strategy to keep them informed and engaged.

To create a communications plan, the team will first identify the stakeholders affected by the project or who have a personal stake in its success. This might include department managers, users of the goods and services, or other parties who will be involved in the project.

The team will then develop a strategy for keeping the stakeholders informed and engaged throughout the project. This might involve establishing regular meetings or check-ins with stakeholders or using communication tools such as email or project management software to keep stakeholders informed of the project's progress. The team will also establish processes for responding to questions or concerns from stakeholders and adjust the project's approach, if necessary, to ensure that stakeholders remain engaged and informed.

By creating a communications plan, the project team can ensure that stakeholders are aware of the project and its progress and can provide the support and feedback needed to ensure its success. This can help the project to be more efficient and effective and prevent delays or problems.

The project team will use various communication technologies, models, and methods to keep stakeholders informed and engaged.

The communication technologies that might be used include:

Email: Email is a standard communication tool used to send updates and information to stakeholders or facilitate discussions and collaboration.

Project management software: Project management software such as Trello or Asana can track progress and provide stakeholders with real-time updates on the project's status.

Video conferencing: Video conferencing tools such as Zoom or Skype can be used to hold virtual meetings with stakeholders or to provide training or support to stakeholders who are located remotely.

The communication models and methods that might be used include:

Two-way communication: This involves actively listening to and engaging with stakeholders and encouraging their feedback and input. This helps build trust and improve collaboration.

Stakeholder analysis: This involves understanding stakeholders' needs, interests, and expectations and tailoring communications to meet those needs. This helps ensure that stakeholders are engaged and informed.

Clear, concise messaging: Clear, concise messaging involves using simple, straightforward language to communicate updates and information to stakeholders. This can help to prevent confusion and misunderstandings.

Using various communication technologies, models, and methods, the project team can ensure that stakeholders are aware of the project and its progress and can provide the support and feedback needed to ensure its success. This can help the project be more efficient and effective and reduce the risk of delays or problems.

RISK MANAGEMENT PLAN

One way to incorporate agile practices into procurement and sourcing project risk-planning is to use agile tools and techniques, such as creating a backlog of procurement and sourcing activities, prioritizing those activities based on their potential impact and the likelihood of occurrence, and regularly reviewing and updating the risk plan as the project progresses.

Another critical aspect of using agile methods for procurement and sourcing project risk-planning is involving all relevant stakeholders in the risk-planning process. This can help ensure that potential risks are identified and addressed early on and that everyone knows their roles and responsibilities in managing them.

Overall, using agile practices for risk planning can help ensure that the project remains on track and can adapt to changes as they arise, leading to a successful outcome.

IDENTIFY RISKS

Potential risks can arise during a procurement and sourcing project, and using agile methods for risk planning can help identify and address those risks promptly and effectively. Common risks that may be identified during the risk planning process include:

Incomplete or inaccurate requirements: If the requirements for the procurement and sourcing project are not clear and subject to change, this can lead to delays, cost overruns, and other issues.

Delays in delivery or payment: If suppliers cannot deliver goods or services on time or if payment is not made on time, this leads to delays and disruptions in the project.

Changes in market conditions: Market conditions can change rapidly, which can lead to issues such as cost increases or reduced availability of goods and services.

Inadequate communication: Poor communication can lead to misunderstandings and misalignment among stakeholders, which can cause delays and other issues in the procurement and sourcing project.

Ineffective risk management: If the risk management plan is ineffective, risks may not be identified and addressed promptly with potential procurement and sourcing project issues.

By using agile tools and techniques and involving all relevant stakeholders in the risk-planning process, these and other risks can be identified and addressed early on, helping to ensure the success of the procurement and sourcing project.

PERFORM QUALITATIVE RISK ANALYSIS

Qualitative risk analysis is a process used to evaluate and prioritize risks based on their potential impact and likelihood of occurrence. This process can be useful during procurement and sourcing project risk-planning because it allows for a systematic and comprehensive evaluation of the risks that may arise during the project.

To perform qualitative risk analysis during the procurement and sourcing project risk-planning using agile methods, all the potential risks that may arise during the procurement and sourcing project must be identified. This can be done through a brainstorming session with all relevant stakeholders or by reviewing the project plan and identifying potential risk areas.

Risks should be assessed based on their likelihood and potential impact once identified. This can be done by assigning a likelihood and impact rating to each risk, such as "high likelihood/high impact" or "low likelihood/low impact."

After the likelihood and impacts of the risks have been identified, it is possible to prioritize them so that the most significant risks can be addressed first. This can be done by creating a risk matrix that shows the likelihood and impact of each risk and using that information to prioritize the risks.

The next step is to develop plans for how to deal with the risks after they have been prioritized. The risk can be reduced by taking preventative measures or developing contingency plans for when it occurs.

By performing qualitative risk analysis during the procurement and sourcing project risk-planning, potential risks can be identified, assessed, and prioritized, allowing for more effective and efficient risk management throughout the project.

PERFORM QUANTITATIVE RISK ANALYSIS

Quantitative risk analysis is a process that uses mathematical models and calculations to evaluate the potential impact of identified risks on a project. This type of analysis is typically used during the risk-planning phase of a procurement and sourcing project to identify the most significant risks and to prioritize the allocation of resources to manage those risks.

To perform a quantitative risk analysis during the risk-planning phase of an agile procurement and sourcing project, follow these steps:

- Identify the risks that have been identified during the risk identification phase of the project.
- Determine the probability and impact of each identified risk. A probability and impact matrix can be used to visually assess a risk's potential impact on a project.
- Use a mathematical model or calculation to determine the expected value of each identified risk. The expected value is the product of the probability and impact of a risk.
- Rank the identified risks in terms of their expected value, with the highest expected value risks being the most significant.

- Develop a risk response plan to address the most significant risks and reduce their expected value or mitigate their impact.

It is important to note that quantitative risk analysis is one of the approaches to risk management in an agile procurement and sourcing project. Other approaches, such as qualitative risk analysis and mitigation, may also be used to manage risks in an agile project.

SOURCING MANAGEMENT PLAN

A procurement and sourcing project plan for an agile project should be flexible and adaptable to changes, as agile projects often involve a high degree of uncertainty and change. The program should also be focused on achieving the project's goals and objectives and should include the following elements:

- a clear statement of the project's goals and objectives, including the project's desired outcomes and the benefits that it is expected to provide
- a description of the project's scope, including the specific procurement and sourcing activities that will be performed and the stakeholders who will be involved
- a detailed project schedule, including each stage's key milestones and deliverables
- a budget and resource plan, including the estimated costs of the procurement and sourcing activities and the

personnel and other resources that will be needed to complete the project

- a risk management plan, including an assessment of the potential risks that may affect the project and a strategy for managing those risks
- a communication plan, including the mechanisms that will be used to keep stakeholders informed about the project's progress and to obtain their feedback and input.

Overall, an effective procurement and sourcing project plan for an agile project should focus on achieving the project's goals and objectives and be flexible and adaptable to changes to maximize the project's chances of success.

STAKEHOLDERS ENGAGEMENT PLAN

A procurement and sourcing stakeholders engagement plan is a document that outlines the strategies and activities that will be used to engage and involve the stakeholders of a procurement and sourcing project. In an agile project, the stakeholder's engagement plan should be flexible and adaptable to changes, as agile projects often involve a high degree of uncertainty and change.

To develop a stakeholders engagement plan for an agile project, follow these steps:

- Identify the stakeholders. This may include internal stakeholders, such as project team members and managers, and external stakeholders, such as vendors and suppliers.

- Determine the level of involvement and engagement each stakeholder will have in the project. This may include activating input and feedback on the project's goals and objectives, participating in meetings and workshops, and reviewing and approving project deliverables.
- Develop a communication plan. This is used to keep stakeholders informed about the project's progress and to obtain their feedback and input. This may include using communication tools such as email, project management software, and regular project status updates.
- Identify potential risks and issues. This will involve any factors that may affect the engagement and involvement of stakeholders in the project. Strategies should then be developed to mitigate those risks and issues.
- Develop a plan to measure and evaluate the effectiveness of the stakeholder's engagement efforts. This should be adjusted as needed to ensure that the project's stakeholders are effectively engaged and involved.

Overall, an effective procurement and sourcing stakeholders engagement plan for an agile project should be focused on engaging and involving the project's stakeholders in a flexible and adaptable manner to maximize their contribution to the project's success.

KICK-OFF MEETING

In this meeting, the sourcing project manager presents the project management plan to the internal stakeholders and obtains approval from the sponsor or the critical stakeholder to launch the tender.

The procurement and sourcing kick-off meeting is an important event that marks the start of a procurement and sourcing project. This meeting is typically held after the project's plans and preparations have been completed. Its purpose is to introduce the project team and stakeholders formally, review the project's goals and objectives and establish a plan for moving forward.

To conduct a successful procurement and sourcing kick-off meeting using agile principles, follow these steps:

- Invite all the project's stakeholders to attend the meeting, including project team members, managers, vendors, and suppliers.
- Provide an overview of the project's goals and objectives, and review the project's plans and preparations, including the project schedule, budget, and risk management plan.
- Introduce the project team and stakeholders and establish roles and responsibilities for everyone.
- Discuss the project's communication plan and establish the mechanisms that will be used to keep stakeholders informed about the project's progress and to obtain their feedback and input.
- Establish a plan for moving forward with the project, including the specific tasks and activities that will be performed in the coming weeks and months and the milestones and deliverables that will be achieved.
- End the meeting with a discussion of any open issues or concerns and establish a plan for addressing those issues.

Overall, a successful procurement and sourcing kick-off meeting using agile principles should set the stage for a productive and successful project and help establish a clear plan for moving forward.

CHAPTER 4

PROJECT EXECUTION

*EFFECTIVE EXECUTION OF A SOURCING PROJECT
INVOLVES CAREFUL PLANNING AND THE ABIL-
ITY TO ADAPT AND ADJUST AS NECESSARY TO
ACHIEVE THE DESIRED OUTCOMES.*

The sourcing manager or leader will provide clear guidance on the management approach and how urgent the project needs to be when the project management plan is done; the plan of execution starts when the project management plan is done.

When a project is critical, you need to use tools and techniques to get it done faster than other projects that might take longer, so you need to use the entire sourcing plan.

DEVELOPING TENDER DOCUMENTS

Creating tender documents is a crucial step in the procurement process, as it ensures that suppliers clearly understand the requirements and expectations.

In a sourcing tender process, there is a diverse range of documents:

Invitation to tender: This document is issued by the company seeking bids and outlines the details of the goods or services being sought, the deadline for submitting bids, and the evaluation criteria used to select the winning bid.

Request for information (RFI): The company issues this document to potential suppliers to gather information about the goods or services being pursued. The RFI may include questions about the supplier's capabilities, experience, and pricing.

Request for proposal (RFP): This document is like an RFI, but it is typically more detailed and may include specific requirements or preferences that the company has for the goods or services being sought.

Request for quotation (RFQ): This document is issued by the company to potential suppliers and includes details about the goods or services and the quantity and quality requirements. The RFQ may also include information about the delivery schedule and payment terms.

Bid submission form: Potential suppliers use this document to submit their bids in response to the tender. The bid submission form typically includes information about the goods or services offered, pricing, and specific terms or conditions.

Evaluation criteria: This document outlines the specific criteria used to evaluate the bids and select the winning supplier. The evaluation criteria may include price, quality, delivery schedule, and the supplier's experience and capabilities.

Bidder's list: This document lists all potential suppliers who have submitted bids in response to the tender.

Award notice: This document is issued by the company to the winning supplier, informing them that their bid has been accepted. It may include information about the contract terms and any applicable special conditions.

Contract: This document outlines the terms and conditions of the agreement between the company and the winning supplier. The contract may include details such as the scope of work, the delivery schedule, the payment terms, and any performance or quality standards that must be met.

The scope of work will align with the scope management plan; if the tender is related to goods, you must indicate that the shipping costs will be included or excluded depending on the incoterms used.

Incoterms specify the obligations of the seller and the buyer regarding transportation and delivery. Depending on the mode of transportation, the location of the buyer and seller, and the specific requirements of the goods being traded, the incoterm chosen for a particular trade agreement will vary.

There are eleven incoterms, or International Commercial Terms, that are commonly used in international trade:

EXW (ex works): This incoterm means that the seller's only obligation is to make the goods available at their premises (works, factory, warehouse). The buyer is responsible for arranging and paying for the collection and transportation of the goods.

FCA (free carrier): This incoterm requires the seller to deliver the goods at a specified location to a specified carrier. Transporting the goods to their destination is the buyer's responsibility.

FAS (free alongside ship): The seller is responsible for delivering the goods alongside a ship at a specified port of shipment. Loading and transporting the goods to their destination are the buyer's responsibilities.

FOB (free on board): This incoterm is like FAS, but the seller is responsible for loading the goods onto the ship. The buyer is still responsible for paying for the transportation of the goods to their destination.

CFR (cost and freight): This incoterm entails the seller's obligation to pay the transportation costs and freight for the goods. In addition to unloading the goods from the ship, the buyer is responsible for arranging and paying for further transportation.

CIF (cost, insurance, and freight): This incoterm combines CFR with the responsibility of covering the goods during transportation.

CPT (carriage paid to): Under this incoterm, the seller is responsible for paying the costs for transporting the goods to the specified destination. Transport insurance is the responsibility of the buyer.

CIP (carriage and insurance paid to): This is like CPT, but with insurance arranged and paid for by the seller.

DAT (delivered at terminal): The seller is responsible for delivering the goods to a specified terminal at the agreed-upon destination; it is the buyer's responsibility to arrange and pay for unloading the goods.

DAP (delivered at place): A seller is responsible for delivering goods to a specified place. After the goods are unloaded from the transport vehicle and other transportation beyond the specified location has been arranged, the buyer is responsible for unloading the goods.

DDP (delivered duty paid): This incoterm is the most inclusive, as it requires the seller to assume all the risks and costs associated with delivering the goods to the specified destination, including paying any duties or taxes. The buyer is not responsible for additional costs beyond the agreed-upon purchase price of the goods.

LAUNCHING THE TENDER

The launch of a procurement and sourcing tender using an agile methodology is an important event that marks the start of the bidding and evaluation process for a procurement and sourcing project. This event typically involves publishing a request for proposals (RFP) or quotations (RFQ), which invites vendors and suppliers to submit bids or proposals to fulfill the project's requirements.

To launch a procurement and sourcing tender using agile methodology, follow these steps:

- Develop a detailed RFP or RFQ that outlines the project's requirements and expectations, including the scope of work, timeline, and budget.
- Publish the RFP or RFQ in a public forum, such as an online procurement platform like SAP ARIBA, to make it available to potential vendors and suppliers.
- Allow enough time for vendors and suppliers to prepare and submit their bids or proposals. This period may be shorter in an agile project than in a traditional project, as agile projects often have shorter timelines and more flexible requirements.

- Review the bids and proposals received from vendors and suppliers, and evaluate them based on price, quality, and timeliness criteria.

A contract's price and terms and conditions are typically the primary areas of discussion and negotiation. The purchaser and the vendor or supplier will typically try to agree on the price of the goods or services, including the delivery schedule, quality standards, and payment terms.

During the negotiation process, the purchaser may negotiate a lower price for the goods or services offered or seek to negotiate better terms and conditions, such as a longer warranty period or a more flexible delivery schedule. On the other hand, the vendor or supplier may negotiate a higher price or more favorable terms and conditions to maximize their profits and minimize their risks.

To reach an agreement on the contract's price and terms and conditions, both the purchaser and the vendor or supplier may need to compromise and make concessions. This may involve making trade-offs between different elements of the contract, such as the price, the delivery schedule, and the quality standards.

Overall, tender proposal negotiation is an integral part of the procurement and sourcing process and can help to ensure that the final contract is fair and mutually beneficial for both the purchaser and the vendor or supplier. The winning bid or proposal can then be selected and the contract awarded.

The contract award process is the last step in procurement and sourcing and involves selecting a vendor or supplier to fulfill the project's requirements and expectations. This process typically involves reviewing the bids or proposals received in response to a request for proposals (RFP) or quotations (RFQ) and selecting the one that offers the best value for money and meets the project's requirements and expectations.

To award a contract, follow these steps:

- Review the bids or proposals received in response to the RFP or RFQ and evaluate them based on price, quality, and timeliness criteria.
- Select the winning bid or proposal and award the contract to the selected vendor or supplier.
- Notify the other bidders or proposers that their bids or proposals were unsuccessful and provide them with an explanation of the reasons for the decision.
- Update the project stakeholders on the outcome of the contract award process and provide them with information about the selected vendor or supplier and the terms and conditions of the contract.
- Begin work on the contract with the selected vendor or supplier and monitor their performance to ensure that they meet the contract's terms and conditions.

Overall, the contract award process is an integral part of the procurement and sourcing process and helps to ensure that a qualified and capable vendor or supplier provides the project's goods or services. Maintaining transparency and trust involves keeping stakeholders informed about the outcome of this process.

Launching a procurement and sourcing tender using an agile methodology involves a streamlined and flexible process focused on quickly identifying and selecting the best vendor or supplier for the project. This approach ensures that the project's procurement and sourcing activities are completed efficiently and effectively.

RFQ APPROVAL AND AWARD

This stage involves reviewing the bids and proposals received, selecting the best value for money, and meeting the project's requirements and expectations.

Following the selection of the winning bid, the RFQ approval and award process typically consists of the following steps:

- Review the bids and proposals received and evaluate them based on price, quality, and timeliness criteria.
- Select the winning bid or proposal and award the contract to the selected vendor or supplier.
- Notify the other bidders or proposers that their bids or proposals were unsuccessful and provide them with an explanation of the reasons for the decision.
- Update the project stakeholders on the outcome of the RFQ approval and award process and provide them with information about the selected vendor or supplier and the terms and conditions of the contract.
- Begin work on the contract with the selected vendor or supplier and monitor their performance to ensure that they meet the contract's terms and conditions.

Overall, the RFQ approval and award process is an essential part of the procurement and sourcing process and helps to ensure that a qualified and capable vendor or supplier provides the project's goods or services. The outcome of this process should be communicated to stakeholders to maintain transparency and trust.

CHAPTER 5

PROJECT CLOSURE

*THE SUCCESSFUL CLOSING OF A
SOURCING PROJECT IS A TESTAMENT TO
THE HARD WORK AND DEDICATION OF ALL
STAKEHOLDERS INVOLVED AND THE STRONG
PARTNERSHIPS BUILT THROUGHOUT THE PROCESS.*

Once the **RFQ** award approval process is completed, steps should be taken to close the procurement and sourcing project.

These steps are designed to ensure that the project is completed successfully and that all the project's goals and aims have been achieved.

To close a procurement and sourcing project, follow these steps:

- Review the project's performance against its goals and aims and assess whether the project has been successful.
- Conduct a final review of the project's budget and expenses and ensure all the project's costs have been accounted for.
- Conduct a final review of the project's risk management plan and assess the effectiveness of the implemented risk management strategies.

- Conduct a final review of the project's communication plan and ensure that all stakeholders have been informed about the project's progress and outcome.
- Conduct a final review of the project's deliverables and outputs and ensure they meet their requirements and expectations.
- Conduct a final review of the project team's performance and offer feedback and recognition to team members who contributed to the project's success.
- Archive the project's documents and records and ensure they are safely stored and preserved for future reference.
- Communicate the closure to all stakeholders and provide them with information about the project's outcome and any lessons learned.

Overall, closing a procurement and sourcing project involves a thorough review and evaluation of the project's performance and ensures that all the project's goals and aims have been achieved. It is essential to follow these steps carefully to ensure the project's success and the notification of all stakeholders.

UPDATE PROJECT DOCUMENTS

Updating project documents is an essential part of the project management process. It involves regularly reviewing and revising the project's plans and documents to ensure they are correct and current. This can help ensure that the project is managed effectively and that all stakeholders can access the most current information.

To update project documents, follow these steps:

- Identify the documents that need to be updated, such as the project schedule, budget, and risk management plan.
- Review the current versions of the project documents and identify any necessary changes or updates.
- Make the necessary changes and updates to the project documents and ensure they are accurate and complete.
- Share the updated documents with the project team and stakeholders and provide them with any necessary training or support to ensure they can use the updated documents effectively.
- Monitor the use of the updated project documents, and make any additional changes or updates as needed to ensure that they continue to be accurate and relevant.

Overall, updating project documents is an essential part of the project management process and helps to ensure that the project is being managed effectively and that all stakeholders have access to the most current information about the project.

STAKEHOLDERS SURVEY

Conducting a stakeholder survey after the closure of a procurement and sourcing project is a way to gather feedback and insights from stakeholders about the project's performance and outcomes. This survey can provide valuable information and insights that can be used to improve future projects and can help to build trust and engagement with stakeholders.

To conduct a stakeholder's survey after the closure of a procurement and sourcing project, follow these steps:

- Develop a survey questionnaire that includes questions about the project's performance and outcomes and the stakeholders' level of satisfaction and engagement with the project.
- Distribute the survey questionnaire to the project's stakeholders and provide them with clear instructions on completing the survey.
- Collect and analyze the survey responses and identify any trends, patterns, or themes that emerge from the data.
- Prepare a report on the survey findings and share the information with the project team and stakeholders.
- Use the survey findings to identify areas for improvement in future projects and incorporate those improvements into future project plans and processes.
- Share the survey findings with other teams and organizations and encourage them to use the information to improve their projects.

Overall, conducting a stakeholder survey after the closure of a procurement and sourcing project can provide valuable insights and feedback that can be used to improve future projects. Engaging stakeholders in the survey process and using the survey findings to drive continuous improvement in future projects is essential.

HAND OVER THE CONTRACT TO THE SUPPLIER MANAGER

Handing a contract to a supplier manager transfers the contract to the selected vendor or supplier. This typically occurs after the warranty has been awarded and involves providing the supplier manager with all the necessary information and resources to manage the contract effectively.

To hand over a contract to a supplier manager, follow these steps:

- Review the contract and the terms and conditions of the agreement and ensure that the supplier manager is familiar with the details of the contract.
- Provide the supplier manager with necessary information or resources, such as project schedules, budgets, and specifications, to help them manage the contract effectively.
- Establish a communication plan and schedule for ongoing communication with the supplier manager and provide them with regular updates on the project's progress and any changes to the contract.
- Train the supplier manager on any processes or procedures they need to follow to fulfill the contract and provide them with any necessary support or assistance.
- Monitor the supplier manager's performance and provide them with feedback and guidance as needed to help them manage the contract effectively.

Overall, the handover of a contract to a supplier manager is an essential part of the procurement and sourcing process and helps to ensure that the contract is managed effectively and that the project's goals and objectives are achieved. It is essential to provide the supplier manager with the necessary information and support to help them succeed.

UPDATE LESSONS LEARNED (TRANSFER OF KNOWLEDGE)

Lessons learned are documented and shared during a project by updating lessons learned, also known as "transferring knowledge." This way, the knowledge and experience gained during the project can be preserved and used in future projects.

To update lessons learned, follow these steps:

- Identify the key lessons and insights gained during the project, such as successful strategies, challenges and obstacles, and areas for improvement.
- Document the lessons and insights in a lessons-learned report or other format and share the report with the project team and stakeholders.
- Discuss the lessons and insights with the project team and stakeholders and encourage them to share their experiences and perspectives.
- Use the lessons and insights to identify areas for improvement in future projects and incorporate those improvements into future project plans and processes.
- Share the lessons and insights with other teams and organizations and encourage them to use the information to improve their projects.

Two types of knowledge can be shared while updating lessons learned: explicit knowledge and tacit knowledge.

Explicit knowledge can be easily articulated and shared in a formal, written format. This knowledge includes facts, figures, and information that can be easily documented and communicated to others. Examples of explicit knowledge include project schedules, budgets, and specifications.

Tacit knowledge, on the other hand, is knowledge that is difficult to articulate and share in a formal, written format. This knowledge includes individual experiences, insights, and intuitive understandings that are difficult to capture in words. Examples of tacit knowledge include personal insights gained from experience and lessons learned from previous projects.

Both explicit and tacit knowledge are essential for updating lessons learned, as they provide valuable information and insights that can be used to improve future projects. It is essential to document and share both types of knowledge during the lessons-learned process to ensure that the knowledge and experience gained during the project are preserved but used to improve future projects.

THE LESSONS-LEARNED REGISTER

The lessons-learned register is a document or database that records the lessons and insights gained during a project. This document is typically updated regularly as new lessons and insights are achieved. It is used to document and share the knowledge and experience gained during the project.

The lessons-learned register typically includes the following information:

- the key lessons and insights gained during the project, including successful strategies, challenges and obstacles, and areas for improvement
- the specific situations or events that led to the lessons and insights being gained
- the individuals or teams who were responsible for gaining the lessons and insights
- the actions or changes that were implemented because of the lessons and insights
- the impact or outcomes of the lessons and insights on the project's goals and objectives.

The lessons-learned register is typically used as a reference document. Project team members and stakeholders access it to learn from the experiences and insights gained during the project. It can also be used to identify areas for improvement in future projects and to share the knowledge and experience gained during the project with other teams and organizations.

Overall, a lessons-learned register is a valuable tool for capturing and sharing the knowledge and experience gained during a project and can help to improve future projects' efficiency and effectiveness.

LESSONS-LEARNED REPOSITORY

All lessons and insights gained from all projects are stored and shared in a lessons-learned repository, which is designed to act as a database of information for when similar projects are undertaken in the future.

Overall, updating lessons learned is an integral part of the project management process and helps to ensure that the knowledge and experience gained during the project are preserved and used to improve future projects. This can increase future projects' efficiency and effectiveness and improve outcomes and results.

PROJECT CLOSURE

A procurement and sourcing project is closed once all its activities, tasks, deliverables, and outputs have been completed. This process typically consists of conducting a thorough review and evaluation of the project's performance and ensuring that all the project's goals and objectives have been achieved.

To close a procurement and sourcing project, follow these steps:

- Review the project's performance against its goals and objectives and assess whether the project has been successful.
- Conduct a final review of the project's budget and expenses and ensure all the project's costs have been accounted for.

- Conduct a final review of the project's risk management plan and assess the effectiveness of the implemented risk management strategies.
- Conduct a final review of the project's communication plan and ensure that all stakeholders have been informed about the project's progress and outcome.
- Conduct a final review of the project's deliverables and outputs and ensure they meet their requirements and expectations.
- Conduct a final review of the project team's performance and provide feedback and recognition to team members who contributed to the project's success.
- Archive the project's documents and records and ensure they are safely stored and preserved for future reference.
- Communicate the closure to all stakeholders and provide them with information about the project's outcome and any lessons learned.

Overall, closing a procurement and sourcing project involves a thorough review and evaluation of the project's performance and ensures that all the project's goals and objectives have been achieved. It is essential to follow these steps carefully for the project to be completed successfully and for all stakeholders to be informed of its completion. All stakeholders should be informed of the project's completion, and the completion of the project should be successful.

CHAPTER 6

SUSTAINABLE SOURCING

*IN TODAY'S INTERCONNECTED WORLD,
ORGANIZATIONS NO LONGER SEE
SUSTAINABILITY AS A COMPLIANCE OR
REPORTING ISSUE BUT AS A BUSINESS IMPERATIVE.
SUSTAINABILITY IS MORE CRITICAL THAN EVER
FOR YOUR LONG-TERM SUCCESS.*

Sustainable procurement and sourcing are an important part of any business's operations. It is the practice
of buying goods and services produced in a way that is environmentally friendly, socially responsible, and economically
viable. Sustainable procurement and sourcing help businesses
reduce their environmental impact, support local communities,
and create a more sustainable supply chain. The environmental
benefits of sustainable procurement and sourcing are clear: by
sourcing goods and services from suppliers that use renewable
energy, reduce waste, and use fewer resources, businesses can
reduce their carbon footprint and help protect the environment.

Sustainable procurement and sourcing can also help businesses reduce their water and energy consumption, which
can lead to cost savings. Sustainable procurement and sourcing also have social benefits. By sourcing goods and services
from local suppliers, businesses can help support their local

communities and create jobs. Additionally, businesses can use sustainable procurement and sourcing to ensure that their suppliers treat their workers fairly and provide safe working conditions. Finally, sustainable procurement and sourcing can help businesses save money overall. Businesses can reduce their energy and water costs by sourcing goods and services from suppliers that use renewable energy and reduce waste.

Additionally, businesses can use sustainable procurement and sourcing to ensure that their suppliers provide quality goods and services at competitive prices. In conclusion, sustainable procurement and sourcing are important to any business's operations, helping them to reduce their environmental impact, support local communities, and create a more sustainable supply chain. Additionally, businesses can save money overall by reducing their energy and water costs and ensuring that their suppliers are providing quality goods and services at competitive prices.

SUSTAINABLE SOURCING POLICY

A sustainable sourcing policy is a set of guidelines and practices that an organization puts in place to ensure that the goods and services it purchases are obtained in an environmentally and socially responsible manner. This can include choosing suppliers who use sustainable manufacturing processes, promoting the use of recycled materials, and considering the overall environmental impact of a product or service throughout its lifecycle.

A sustainable sourcing policy is important because it can help organizations to reduce their environmental footprint and support the development of sustainable practices in their supply chain. By implementing a sustainable sourcing policy, an organization can positively contribute to the environment and help create a more sustainable future.

SUSTAINABLE SOURCING POLICY EXAMPLE

A sustainable sourcing policy might include the following:

1. The company will only source materials and products from suppliers who are committed to ethical and sustainable practices.
2. The company will conduct regular audits of its suppliers to ensure that they are meeting its standards.
3. The company will only source materials and products from suppliers who are committed to reducing their environmental impact.
4. The company will only source materials and products from suppliers who are committed to fair labor practices.
5. The company will only source materials and products from suppliers who are committed to the responsible sourcing of raw materials.
6. The company will only source materials and products from suppliers who are committed to reducing their carbon footprint.

7. The company will only source materials and products from suppliers who are committed to reducing their water usage.
8. The company will only source materials and products from suppliers who are committed to reducing their waste.
9. The company will only source materials and products from suppliers who are committed to reducing their energy usage.
10. The company will only source materials and products from suppliers who are committed to reducing their chemical usage.
11. The company will only source materials and products from suppliers who are committed to reducing their packaging.
12. The company will only source materials and products from suppliers who are committed to reducing their transportation costs.
13. The company will only source materials and products from suppliers who are committed to reducing their emissions.
14. The company will only source materials and products from suppliers who are committed to reducing their water pollution.
15. The company will only source materials and products from suppliers who are committed to reducing their air pollution.
16. The company will only source materials and products from suppliers who are committed to reducing their hazardous waste.
17. The company will only source materials and products from suppliers who are committed to reducing their use of hazardous chemicals.

18. The company will only source materials and products from suppliers who are committed to reducing their use of genetically modified organisms.
19. The company will only source materials and products from suppliers who are committed to reducing their use of animal products.
20. The company will only source materials and products from suppliers who are committed to reducing their use of palm oil.

By implementing a sustainable sourcing policy, companies can ensure that their suppliers are meeting their standards and that their products are being sourced from ethical and sustainable sources. This helps to protect the environment, reduce the company's carbon footprint, and ensure that the company is doing its part to promote sustainability.

SUSTAINABLE SOURCING STANDARD

Sustainable sourcing standards provide guidelines for organizations to use when evaluating the sustainability of goods and services they purchase.

These standards may include recycled content requirements, sustainable manufacturing practices, and carbon reduction goals. The development of sustainable practices in the supply chain can be supported by using sustainable sourcing standards to assist organizations in making informed and responsible purchasing decisions. Sustainable sourcing standards can help organizations create a more sustainable future.

SUSTAINABLE SOURCING STANDARD EXAMPLE

One example of a sustainable sourcing standard is the Responsible Sourcing Standard (RSS). This standard was developed by the Responsible Business Alliance (RBA) and is based on human rights, labor rights, environmental protection, and anti-corruption principles. The RSS requires companies to assess their suppliers and ensure they meet the standards set forth by the RBA. Companies must also develop and implement a responsible sourcing policy and train their suppliers on the standards.

The RSS also requires companies to monitor their suppliers and take corrective action if any issues are found. Companies must also report on their progress in meeting the standards and provide evidence of their compliance. The RSS also requires companies to have a grievance mechanism to address any issues that arise.

The RSS is a crucial tool for companies to ensure that their sourcing practices are sustainable. By following the standards set forth by the RBA, companies can ensure that their suppliers are meeting the highest standards of social and environmental responsibility. This helps to ensure that the materials, products, and services that companies source are produced in a way that is socially and environmentally responsible.

SUSTAINABLE SOURCING PROCEDURE

The sustainable sourcing process begins with the identification of potential suppliers who meet the company's sustainability criteria. This includes assessing the supplier's environmental and social performance, as well as their commitment to ethical practices. Companies should also consider the supplier's ability to meet their needs in terms of quality, cost, and delivery. Once potential suppliers have been identified, the company should conduct a thorough evaluation of the supplier's sustainability practices. This includes assessing the supplier's environmental and social performance, as well as their commitment to ethical practices.

Once a supplier has been selected, the company should develop a sustainable sourcing agreement with the supplier. This agreement should outline the company's expectations for the supplier's sustainability practices, as well as the supplier's commitment to meeting those expectations. The agreement should also include a timeline for the implementation of the sustainable sourcing practices.

The company should also develop a monitoring and reporting system to ensure that the supplier is meeting the company's sustainability expectations. This includes regular audits of the supplier's practices and performance, as well as regular reporting of the supplier's progress. The company should also develop a system for addressing any issues that arise during the monitoring process.

Finally, the company should develop a system for rewarding suppliers who meet the company's sustainability expectations. This could include preferential pricing, longer-term contracts, or other incentives. By rewarding suppliers who meet the company's sustainability expectations, the company can encourage suppliers to continue to improve their sustainability practices.

Sustainable sourcing is an important part of a company's overall sustainability strategy. By following a sustainable sourcing procedure, companies can ensure that the products and services they use are produced in a way that is environmentally friendly and socially responsible.

SUSTAINABLE SOURCING PROCEDURE EXAMPLE

The first step in a sustainable sourcing procedure is to identify the materials and products that need to be sourced. This includes both raw materials and finished products. It is important to consider the environmental impact of each material or product, as well as the social and economic implications of sourcing from certain suppliers. Once the materials and products have been identified, the next step is to research potential suppliers. This includes looking into their sustainability practices, such as their commitment to ethical labor practices, their use of renewable energy sources, and their efforts to reduce waste and emissions.

Once potential suppliers have been identified, the next step is to evaluate them. This includes assessing their ability to meet the business's sustainability goals, as well as their ability to provide quality products and services. It is also important to consider the cost of the materials and products, as well as the potential for long-term savings. Once the evaluation is complete, the business can then select the most suitable supplier.

The last step in a sustainable sourcing procedure example is to monitor the supplier's performance. This includes regularly assessing the supplier's sustainability practices, as well as their ability to meet the business's sustainability goals. It is also important to ensure that the supplier is meeting the agreed-upon delivery times and quality standards. Regular monitoring of the supplier's performance will help ensure that the business is getting the most out of its sustainable sourcing efforts.

Sustainable sourcing is an important part of any business's operations. A sustainable sourcing procedure can help businesses ensure that their sourcing practices are in line with their sustainability goals. By maintaining a sustainable sourcing procedure, businesses can ensure that they are sourcing materials and products from suppliers who are committed to ethical and sustainable practices, while also ensuring that they are getting the most out of their sustainable sourcing efforts.

CHAPTER 7

SUPPLIER MANAGEMENT

*ALL PROJECTS ARE DEPENDENT UPON
SUPPLIERS; YOU SHOULD DEVOTE ENOUGH TIME
AND ENERGY TO EACH SUPPLIER BASED ON THE
STRATEGIC IMPORTANCE THEY HOLD.*

The effective management of suppliers ensures that all sourcing efforts will be well-spent so that long-term relationships can be built with them, and the process of finding alternative suppliers every time one fails is significantly reduced.

Supplier management involves managing and coordinating suppliers' activities to ensure that they provide the goods and services that a business needs in a timely and cost-effective manner. This can involve collaborating closely with suppliers to understand their capabilities and capacity, negotiating contracts and pricing, and monitoring their performance to ensure they meet the business's expectations.

The management of suppliers is a crucial part of supply chain management, which coordinates the flow of goods and services. Effective supplier management can help a business reduce costs, improve the quality of its goods and services, and ensure a steady supply of the materials and components it needs to operate.

A business typically develops and maintains a supplier information database to manage its suppliers effectively, including contact details, capabilities, capacity, and performance history. This information can be used to select appropriate suppliers, negotiate contracts, and monitor their performance. The business may also establish formal agreements with its suppliers, outlining the terms and conditions of their relationship and any performance metrics that will be used to evaluate their performance.

In addition to managing its existing suppliers, a business may also need to identify and evaluate potential new suppliers to meet increased demand or replace existing suppliers who need to meet the business's needs. This can involve researching to identify potential suppliers, contacting them to request information and quotes, and evaluating their responses to determine which suppliers are the best fit for the business.

Effective supplier management is an important part of a successful business operation. It involves developing and maintaining relationships with suppliers, negotiating contracts, and ensuring that the business has access to the goods and services it needs to operate efficiently and effectively.

MANAGING SUPPLIERS

There are key steps involved in managing suppliers effectively:

Identifying and selecting suppliers: This involves identifying the goods and services the business needs and identifying potential suppliers who can provide them. In addition to price, quality, and delivery times, you should also consider the supplier's reputation and history.

Negotiating contracts: Once a supplier has been identified, the next step is to negotiate a contract that outlines the terms of the relationship, including the prices and quantities of goods or services to be provided, delivery times, and any other relevant terms.

Managing the relationship: After the contract has been signed, it is important to maintain strong relationships with suppliers. This involves regular communication, prompt payment, and resolving any issues.

Monitoring and evaluating supplier performance: It is important to regularly review supplier performance to ensure that they meet the contract terms and that the business is getting the best value for its money.

WHAT IS SUPPLIER MANAGEMENT?

Supplier management involves systematically identifying, evaluating, and establishing mutually beneficial supplier relationships.

Collaboration with suppliers can help an organization achieve greater efficiency and competitive advantage. In addition, it allows an organization to receive the highest possible value from its suppliers.

Suppliers and organizations need to operate efficiently to succeed financially and operationally.

A strong supplier relationship can lead to savings for organizations, increase value, and help them accomplish their strategic goals.

Supplier relationships are determined by the service they provide. When a supplier is not critical to the business or it is an inventory stock item, you do not have to spend time managing it. However, when a supplier is essential to the business strategically, time will need to be spent on strengthening the relationship.

DEVELOP POLICIES, STANDARDS, AND PROCEDURES

Organizations need clear guidelines to manage their relationships with suppliers, including:

A sourcing policy: A high-level statement that incorporates the goals, intentions, beliefs, and governing principles that define how a company will fulfill its obligations (legal, ethical, contractual).

A sourcing standard: A set of mandatory rules that defines the technical and minimum acceptable criteria for the performance of processes or the management of risks, against which KPIs can be measured.

A sourcing procedure: Step-by-step instructions for achieving a specific goal or mandate, as well as the process, roles, and responsibilities for practical sourcing activities.

WHO MANAGES SUPPLIER RELATIONS?

A procurement or sourcing manager does not necessarily need to manage this role; a procurement leader, logistics manager, or business unit manager could do it. However, the procurement or sourcing manager must be the one to guide and manage the supplier's managers.

SUPPLIER LIFECYCLE MANAGEMENT

In supplier lifecycle management (SLM), external suppliers are managed transparently, organized, and integrated.

Suppliers are placed at the heart of an organization's procurement process and strategy to recognize the value they provide.

The following image portrays the lifecycle, starting from onboarding, then progressing to the development plan and suppliers' engagement or phase out due to deficient performance or any other issues.

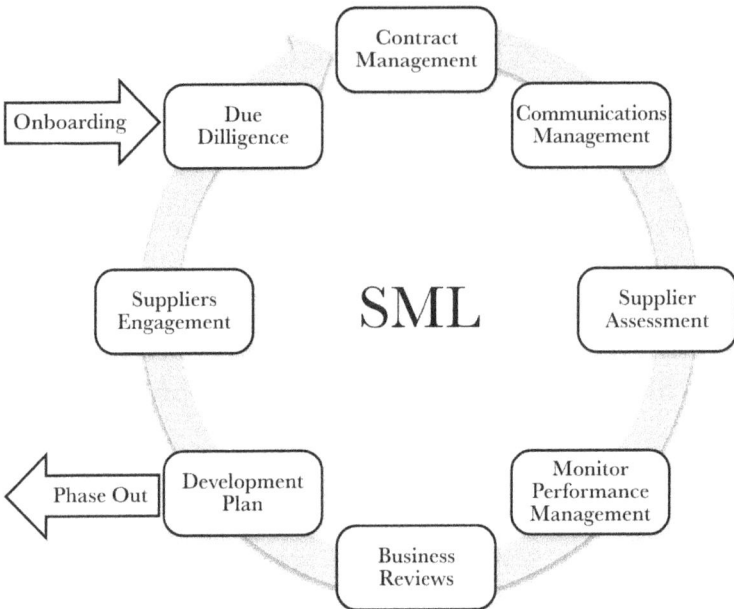

IMAGE 1

Strategic sourcing identifies, assesses, and selects suppliers that can satisfy the organization's long-term needs.

This can involve researching to identify potential suppliers, assessing their capabilities and capacity, and negotiating contracts and pricing to ensure that the business receives the goods and services it needs in a timely and cost-effective manner.

A supplier development plan is a document or strategy that outlines the steps and activities a business will take to support and improve the performance of its suppliers. This can involve collaborating with suppliers to identify areas for improvement.

Geller & Company's whitepaper illustrates how poor supplier performance management can erode strategic sourcing savings.

Value Capture from Sourcing Depends on How Well Companies Manage Suppliers

Impact of Supplier Engagement Strategies

Illustrative

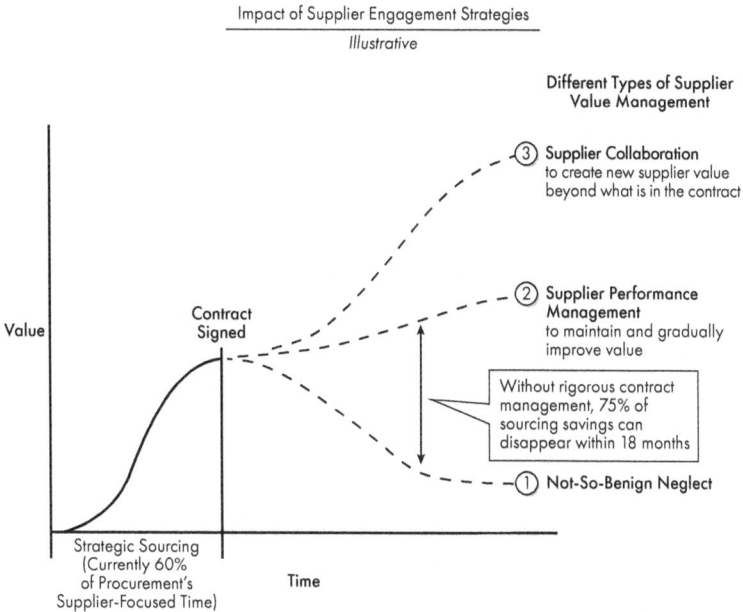

IMAGE 2

Source: Geller & Company, "World-Class Procurement—Increasing Profitability and Quality," 2003

Establishing performance metrics and targets can aid in monitoring their progress and providing training or other resources to help them improve.

Developing strategic relationships with suppliers and ensuring access to the goods and services that a business needs to operate effectively and efficiently can help a business build strong, productive relationships.

The business can identify and select the best suppliers with the help of strategic sourcing, while a supplier development plan can support their ongoing growth and improvement. This combination will help a business build a robust and resilient supply chain that will support its long-term success.

SUPPLIER ONBOARDING

Supplier onboarding is the process of bringing new suppliers into an organization's supply chain. This typically involves verifying the supplier's credentials and capabilities, negotiating contract terms, and setting up processes for communication and collaboration.

The goal of supplier onboarding is to ensure that the new supplier can provide the goods or services that the organization needs reliably and cost-effectively. This process is typically managed by an organization's procurement or supply chain management team.

Supplier onboarding is an essential part of managing an organization's supply chain, as it helps to ensure that the organization has access to the goods and services it needs to operate effectively.

Identifying potential suppliers involves identifying companies that can provide the goods or services the organization needs and evaluating their capabilities to ensure they are a good fit for the organization. By carefully vetting potential suppliers and setting up processes for collaboration and communication, organizations can minimize the risk of supply chain disruptions and improve their overall supply chain efficiency.

Onboarding can be influenced by a company's size and complexity, as well as the nature of its procurement needs. In most cases, there are key steps involved in the process:

Verifying supplier credentials: Before bringing a new supplier on board, it is essential to verify their credentials to ensure that they are reputable and capable of providing the goods or services that the organization needs. This typically involves conducting background checks and reviewing references from other customers.

Negotiating contract terms: Once a supplier has been selected, the organization will typically negotiate contract terms with the supplier. This may involve discussing pricing, delivery schedules, and other terms and conditions of the agreement.

Setting up processes for collaboration and communication: To ensure that the relationship with the new supplier is successful, it is essential to establish clear processes for communication and cooperation. This may involve setting up regular meetings or conference calls to discuss issues or concerns and establishing protocols for reporting and resolving problems.

In general, supplier onboarding involves integrating new suppliers into an organization's supply chain in an efficient, cost-effective, and risk-free manner. By managing this process carefully, organizations can ensure they have access to the goods and services they need to operate effectively.

CONTRACT MANAGEMENT

Supplier contract management is the process of overseeing and managing the contracts that an organization has with its suppliers. This typically involves negotiating contract terms, monitoring performance against the contract terms, and making any necessary adjustments to the contract to ensure that it continues to meet the organization's needs.

Supplier contract management ensures that the organization's contracts with its suppliers are effective, efficient, and aligned with its strategic goals. This can help to minimize the risk of supply chain disruptions and improve the organization's overall supply chain efficiency.

The steps involved in supplier contract management can vary depending on the organization's size and complexity and the products or services being procured. In general, though, the process typically involves key steps:

Negotiating contract terms: This involves collaborating with the supplier to establish the terms of the contract, including pricing, delivery schedules, and other key terms and conditions.

Monitoring supplier performance: Once the contract is in place, it is essential to monitor the supplier's performance to ensure that they meet the contract's terms. This may involve tracking delivery times and the quality of goods or services and acting if the supplier needs to make a change to meet the agreed-upon terms.

Managing contract amendments: As the organization's needs change over time, it may be necessary to amend the contract to ensure that it continues to meet its needs. This may involve negotiating changes to the contract with the supplier and updating the contract documentation to reflect the changes.

It is critical to the success of an organization's supply chain that supplier contracts are managed effectively. Supply chain disruptions can be minimized, and the efficiency of the supply chain can be improved by carefully managing contracts with suppliers.

SUPPLIER PROFILE AND ASSESSMENT

A supplier's performance must be monitored over time to ensure they meet the business's expectations and requirements.

To accomplish this, performance metrics and targets can be set, data can be collected on the supplier's performance, and this data can be compared with the metrics and targets.

Monitoring supplier performance can help a business identify any issues with a supplier and take corrective action, if necessary. It may involve collaborating with the supplier to address any issues or concerns, renegotiating contracts or terms and conditions, or even terminating the relationship.

Monitoring a supplier's performance can also help identify areas for improvement and cost-saving opportunities. Negotiating lower prices with suppliers for businesses that consistently meet or exceed their performance targets is possible.

Supplier monitoring helps a business maintain strong and productive relationships with its suppliers, ensuring timely and cost-effective access to the goods and services it needs.

MONITORING PERFORMANCE MANAGEMENT

Supplier management monitoring involves tracking and evaluating a supplier's performance over time to ensure that they meet the business's expectations and requirements. This can involve setting performance metrics and targets, collecting data on the supplier's performance, and comparing this data to the established metrics and targets.

TARGET-SETTING AND BUSINESS REVIEWS

Supplier management target-setting involves establishing specific, measurable, achievable, relevant, and time-bound (SMART) goals and objectives for a supplier's performance and communicating these to the supplier. This helps align the expectations and requirements of the business with the capabilities and capacity of the supplier. It also provides a clear framework for evaluating the supplier's performance.

Key performance indicators (KPIs) are metrics or measures used to track and evaluate a supplier's performance against established targets. Common KPIs in supplier management may include delivery time, order accuracy, product quality, and cost.

Setting targets and KPIs for a supplier's performance can help a business to monitor the supplier's performance over time, identify areas for improvement, and take corrective action, if necessary. This can help ensure that the supplier meets the business's expectations and requirements and can provide opportunities for cost savings and improved efficiency.

Business–supplier relationships can be strengthened through effective target-setting and KPI tracking, ensuring businesses can get their goods and services promptly and cost-effectively.

SUPPLIER DEVELOPMENT PLAN

Supplier development plans describe how businesses support their suppliers and improve their performance through various activities. By collaborating with suppliers, you can identify areas for improvement, provide training and other resources to help them improve, and establish performance metrics and targets to track their progress.

Implementing a supplier development plan can improve the quality of a business's goods and services. In addition to providing cost savings, it can also improve efficiency. The importance of this may be greater for businesses with complex supply chains or fewer suppliers.

Developing a supplier development plan typically involves assessing the supplier's strengths and weaknesses and collaborating with the supplier to develop action plans and implementation strategies.

This may involve setting performance targets, providing training or other support, and establishing regular communication and feedback mechanisms to track progress and identify any issues that need to be addressed.

Supplier development plans can help businesses develop positive relationships with their suppliers and ensure access to the goods and services they need to operate efficiently and effectively.

SUPPLIER ENGAGEMENT

Supplier engagement is building and maintaining solid and productive relationships with a business's suppliers. This can involve regular communication and collaboration, as well as developing strategies and processes to support the supplier's performance and growth.

Effective supplier engagement can help a business improve the quality and reliability of the goods and services it receives from its suppliers. It can also provide opportunities for cost savings and increased efficiency. This can be particularly important for businesses with complex or specialized supply chain needs or those that rely heavily on a small group of key suppliers.

To engage effectively with suppliers, a business may need to establish regular communication channels, such as regular meetings or newsletters, to stay informed about the supplier's capabilities and capacity. The company may also need to provide support and resources to help the supplier improve, such as training or access to technology or equipment.

In addition, a business may need to develop strategies and processes to support the growth and development of its suppliers, such as a supplier development plan or a supplier diversity program. These initiatives help to build long-term, mutually beneficial relationships between the business and its suppliers.

The most effective supplier engagement can enable a company to establish and maintain strong relationships with its suppliers and ensure access to the goods and services it requires for its operations.

CRITICALITY

In supplier management, criticality refers to the importance or significance of a particular supplier to the business. A supplier may be considered critical if the goods or services they provide are essential for the business's operation or if the business has a high dependency on the supplier for a particular product or service.

Determining the criticality of a supplier can help a business to prioritize its efforts and resources in managing its relationships with its suppliers. For example, a business may prioritize developing and improving its relationships with critical suppliers. It may also mitigate any potential risks associated with these suppliers.

To assess the criticality of a supplier, a business may use a variety of factors, such as the strategic importance of the goods or services they provide, the extent of the business's dependency on the supplier, and the potential impact on the business if the supplier were unable to meet its needs. The business may also consider other factors, such as the supplier's financial stability, the quality of their goods and services, and their performance history.

Managing a business's relationships with its suppliers effectively and ensuring that it can get the goods and services it needs to operate effectively and efficiently can be enhanced by understanding the criticality of a supplier.

MANAGED SPEND

Managed spend refers to the sum of a business's money spent on goods and services from its suppliers.

Among the costs involved are direct and indirect spending, such as the cost of raw materials, finished goods, and other supplies, and indirect costs, such as transportation and logistics.

Managed spending is essential in supplier management because it can provide insight into the business's overall spending on goods and services and its dependency on specific suppliers. By understanding its managed spend, a company can identify opportunities for cost savings and efficiencies and develop strategies to reduce its dependence on any single supplier.

To manage its spending effectively, a business may need to develop and maintain a detailed database of its spending on goods and services from its suppliers. This can involve tracking and categorizing spending according to supplier, product or service, and other relevant factors.

The business may also need to develop policies and procedures for managing its spending, such as procurement and contract management processes.

The concept of managed spending can help a business understand its overall spending on goods and services and identify opportunities to save money.

CONCLUSION

An important aspect of business operations is supplier management, which involves identifying, selecting, negotiating, managing, and evaluating suppliers.

Business supplier management ensures that the business has access to the goods and services to operate efficiently and effectively while maintaining strong relationships with its suppliers.

Businesses can improve their efficiency, reduce costs, and increase competitiveness by managing their suppliers effectively.

AUTHOR BIO

Yasser Ismail is a seasoned professional with over 25 years of experience in the oilfield services industry, excelling in accounting, logistics, project management, and supply chain management. Demonstrating strong leadership, Yasser has managed $2B in annual global logistics spending, driving cost savings through strategic sourcing and procurement.

Yasser holds two distinguished certifications from the Project Management Institute: Project Management Professional (PMP) and Certified Agile Practitioner (PMI-ACP). These credentials showcase his dedication to delivering exceptional results.

In addition to his professional accomplishments, Yasser is a passionate entrepreneur with a keen interest in innovation and smart solutions. He has founded and led multiple ventures, such as NFC FZ LLE and Near Range, focusing on Near Field Communication (NFC) technology. Yasser's entrepreneurial spirit and creative problem-solving skills enable him to stay at the forefront of technological advancements.

Balancing his industry experience and entrepreneurial drive, Yasser Ismail continues to make significant contributions in the field of technology, shaping the future through his innovative endeavours. With a diverse skill set and a forward-thinking mindset, Yasser is a true force in the world of business and technology. To learn more about Yasser and his accomplishments, visit his website at https://www.yasserismail.com.

REFERENCES

(n.d.). Retrieved from http://agilemanifesto.org/: http://agilemanifesto.org/iso/en/principles.html.

Full Comparison: Agile vs Scrum vs Waterfall vs Kanban—Smartsheet. (n.d.). Retrieved from https://www.smartsheet.com/agile-vs-scrum-vs-waterfall-vs-kanban.

Highsmith, J. (2001). *Manifesto for Agile Software Development.* Retrieved from Manifesto for Agile Software: http://agilemanifesto.org/history.html.

Institute, P. M. (2017). *A guide to the project management body of knowledge (PMBOK guide).* Pennsylvania: Project Management Institute.

What Is the Difference Between Procurement and Sourcing?. (n.d.) Retrieved from Dryden Group: https://drydengroup.com/procurement-vs-sourcing/.

NOTES

....

....

....

....

....

....

....

....

....

....

....

....

....